VOICE CLOUDS

By

Barbara J. Gunsolley

Bloomington, IN  Milton Keynes, UK

authorHOUSE®

AuthorHouse™
1663 Liberty Drive, Suite 200
Bloomington, IN 47403
www.authorhouse.com
Phone: 1-800-839-8640

AuthorHouse™ UK Ltd.
500 Avebury Boulevard
Central Milton Keynes, MK9 2BE
www.authorhouse.co.uk
Phone: 08001974150

First published by AuthorHouse 12/28/2006

ISBN: 978-1-4259-6352-1 (sc)

Printed in the United States of America
Bloomington, Indiana

This book is printed on acid-free paper.

In the early 1990's when, "the Vacuum Cleaner Revelation,"_ was being written, the environment within the; United States of America, was one of concern with internal violence, such as, the; "Oklahoma Bombing."

Now in 2006, this nation is being forced to fight a global war, caused by terrorists, who are influenced by religious beliefs. This future was a prophetic warning within the text of; "The Vacuum Cleaner Revelation," written by Barbara J. Gunsolley.

Table of Contents

1. A LONG TIME AGO

A long tome ago....there lived a young girl who wanted desperately to be loved by that special man and live happily ever after. However, this fairy tale failed because of the lack of interest from her new lover.

After a short marriage and the births of three children I got a divorce. My husband had an affair and I did not have the emotional stability or desire to stay married. I was only 23 years old and emotionally sick. I escaped through the pursuit of happiness in the bars at night expecting to meet Mr. Right. This was not obvious to me at the time but it was a demonic trap to keep me in a habit of destructive behavior. Trust me on this one there never was a Mr. Right.

The man that I did meet however was the dashing hero of my dreams. I was completely smitten and addicted to being with him. He was good to my children and I became pregnant with my fourth child.

Our relationship was tumultuous. We were separated for a long time after he abandoned us in Denver. He said that he tried to get back but his truck broke down on the way.

He surprised me as he sat on a bar stool where I was working after about two years. I was thrilled to see him. I was supporting my children doing waitress work and getting a housing allowance for low income families.

We connected and continued our road of destruction. I had developed an affinity for the occult. I was reading tarot cards supposedly telling fortunes. I sincerely wanted to be a good fortune teller but I was not confident in what I was doing.

Again our explosive personalities erupted and he left. He called and asked that we reconcile and go to his home state. So I addictively made plans to move. He sent me the money so I and three of my children drove to where he lived. We rented a mobile home and began to live together as a family again.

I now know that the decision to join him again was a disaster waiting to happen and God tried to stop me.

I knew of God as I grew and attended a Catholic School. But I had long sense left Him except for the times when I would argue while in an intoxicated condition and defend Him as if He needed my support.

But now things were changing fast. My aunt who was a Catholic nun had become what is known as "Charismatic." That means that she was now moving in the fullness of the Holy Spirit with evidence of speaking in tongues, interpretation of tongues, prophecy, healings, etc. She invited me to attend a prayer meeting and I was very much impressed. I knew this was where I needed to be but I wanted my man more so I blew it off.

When he first left me again I went to a fortune teller. For those of us who are lost, lonely and desperate and don't know any better we think that we can get comfort from a fortune teller if they tell us what we want to hear. The death card was drawn while I was there so I was told that there would be a death. As you read further you will find that indeed this did happen. And are you getting the picture of how demonic forces and the forces of God are fighting for our souls?

God tried hard to reach me through a dream before I left town. The dream invaded my sleep with prophetic warnings of destruction if I did not reconsider and stay where I was. I did not heed the warning.

I took my family and left for another go around with my man. You have to know that my aunt and her company of prayer warriors were praying for my salvation. I did not know this at that time but I am so glad now that they did.

We were reunited again and happy to be together for a short time until the bars and drunkenness devoured our family life. I became pregnant again. It was rare when we got together sexually but this night he seemed to be proving something to someone because he took me along with him to the bar which was unusual and bragged that we would be having sex later. It just happened that this very night my birth control medication ran empty. From the perspective of what I know now the demonic forces were setting me up for the slaughter.

Now I was pregnant and miserable. He came home late one night because the police were following him and if I had not let him in the door he would have been arrested. I reminded him that I was pregnant and couldn't we make things work? He told me to get an abortion. I lost control and hit him with a heavy fry pan. He did not attack me back he must have understood my turmoil.

So now I am flying back to my original home destination with my children to start all over again but now I am pregnant. I went to the abortion clinic. While I was under the influence of the anesthetic I screamed from deep within a drug induced coma. It took years of God's love to get me through to a healing from this event.

Now I was ready to give up my man. How low did I need to go to reach bottom? I went to the prayer meetings with my aunt and I was completely submerged in the baptism of the Holy Spirit and God's forgiveness and goodness.

I renounced all my affiliations with the occult or anything that I was knowingly or unknowingly doing that was demonic. And God filled me with His presence and gifts.

The child of this union, a girl, has grown to adulthood and she is an outstanding example of the goodness of God. She has a bachelors degree, is married to an awesome Christian man and she and her husband are attending seminary to become ministers. She tells people where ever she goes about Jesus. She has not seen her father since she was four years old.

2. PROPHETIC BEGINNING

Now I am is free from the demonic stronghold of "my man." My first challenge was getting housing and money to support my children. I am attending prayer meetings regularly at the same time. I had a job as a waitress again and I am miraculously re-housed in the same public supported "nice" housing project. The only reason that I did not have to stay on a long waiting list is because one of my friends just happened to have taken the job of managing these apartments.

Now I am initiating contact with my twelve year old son who had chosen to stay with his dad rather that go with me to re unite with "my man." He came on weekends and became a part of the healthy activities they would pursue.

The first training that I had in the spiritual realm was to battle my thoughts and to discern from where they came. The Holy Spirit taught me not to "justify my actions" to Him but to be honest, admit mistakes and let Him change me. He told me that I needed not to feel guilty because I was changing with His help and to be patient with myself. So I did the best I could because I was eager to please God.

I attended prayer meetings where the Holy Spirit was freely moving. At one meeting during the time after the worship music when everyone sat silent waiting for the Holy Spirit to speak through one who would be obedient when they sensed His anointing I had this experience:

"I sat frozen with my heart pounding. I could feel God's presence but I was afraid to open my mouth. I had some words inside near where my heart would be located and I heard them over and over again before I finally spoke. 'Please be patient with Me my servant is now ready to speak' are the words that I released into the crowd."

The reaction was one of "awe" they expressed their joy at the words so I felt the ministry that I released was confirmed.

This was the beginning of a prophetic ministry that would grow over the years.

My children attended these meetings also and they were moving in the gifts of the Holy Spirit.

3. JENNA GOES TO COLLEGE

Let's give our main character a name. It makes it easier to write and understand what is happening. Jenna is my name you might know me from other books. (THE VACUUM CLEANER REVELATION & WHERE THE HECK ARE THE ROES?)

I am now attending college and my youngest child goes to day care on campus. I am meeting students, studying and working in the Audio Visual Center on a student work program.

I have made several acquaintances on campus and Jim is one of them. I am outspoken about Jesus everywhere I go so naturally I connect with the Christians. Jim talked like he was a Christian he said that his mother played an organ in church. I am the "Queen of denial" in respect to letting things just passes by. Jim showed me pictures that he had taken. I quickly thumbed through the photos and as I did a pair of bare breasts popped in my face. I just kept looking through the pictures as though I saw nothing.

Jim and I were close enough friends that it was appropriate for me to talk to him about the hay ride for kids that I was organizing. He volunteered to be a part of the transportation department.

The night of the event came and an assortment of eager helpers established their positions except Jim he was absent. The house quickly filled with energetic children. The hay wagon was rented and waiting. I stuffed bags with hot dogs, buns and treats but how could I get everybody and everything to the hay wagon?

My youngest son invited a sweet little girl to the hay ride as his date. She did not live in our complex so her parents drove her to our place.

Remember the focus here is two different spiritual forces at work. I am now under the influence of the demonic as I froze up and panicked. I went into my room and said, "God if you don't do something right now I quite." At that very moment my son came bursting into the room and told me that his girl friend's parents would transport the extra children.

Many years later this little girl became my daughter- in -law and the mother of three grand children. The parents who drove the children that night and I share many holidays.

I was curious as to what Jim's explanation would be. Here is what I discovered. Jim told me that his mother was an active witch and that he had been placing spells directed toward me but I just continued acting even more excited about God. He seemed confused as to why his spells didn't work.

Bust little Jenna's bubble! Wake up! As a new Christian I was protected but the new reality in which I now live includes being diligent and on guard because I am now a target of the demonic.

4. GREAT DECISION

You may have read in one of my other books "Where the Heck are the Roses?" that I was visited by the Holy Spirit when my youngest daughter was born. I was far from God and trapped in a drunken life style but I guess God could see down the road.

This child is now four years old and as I promised God (Then went back to my evil ways) I enrolled her in Kindergarten in the new Christian school being birthed at the church my children and I attended.

I am still going to college and my other children are in a public school. I finished my associate's degree classes and I am transferring to a four year college. But....now I am hearing deep within where Jesus speaks that I was to go to the leadership of the fledging school and volunteer my services. This would mean that I would leave my studies in the middle of a semester. After a great internal struggle I was obedient.

The Superintendent of the school was shocked at my proposal momentarily. Then she said, "We have been praying for God to send people to be a part of the school." I think she was hoping for something more than me but she recognized that it was God who had sent me and I became part of the staff.

By the next school year all of my children were enrolled in the Christian School. We as a family were living rent free on campus and I had a salary to care for my children. These were the most blessed times of our lives. The goodness of God's people poured upon us over and over again over the years and we all grew in relationship with Jesus.

I sacrificed my four year education at the prompting of God and it was the best decision of my life other than hooking up with Jesus.

5. NOT A GREAT DECISION

Now my children and I are living and flourishing in the fertile environment of the church and school campus where we have lived on grounds for several years. I am still hoping and praying for a husband. I belong to a singles group and have developed relationships that allow for us to share on a deep level. Several men and women have met and married during this time.

I am still waiting and honestly quite desperately. This is much different than the old days when I could get a man at the drop of my voice. Now the stakes are higher and my values correspond. The fact that I have four children is surely a deterrent but two mothers with three kids got married.

Do you remember Magnum P.I.? A T.V. program starring Tom Seleck ? The new man in our midst resembled Tom in a dramatic way.

I was amazed and even in denial that he was in pursuit of my attention. As was the custom in the singles group males and females gathered in formally and talked not considering it a date. At one of these meetings Mr. Tom look alike said that he would be making an attempt to connect with a female in the group and I missed the clue that he meant me.

Long story short we married and planned a mission trip to the Philippines. He was a helicopter pilot and he had spoken with missionaries in Europe who needed a pilot.

These plans included my children but my plans were not included in their plans. In other words they were animate that they would not go.

This was not working and I should have got a clue. I wanted desperately to be a missionary but the plans were falling apart and they were not good for my children.

Also, I was getting a full does of the personality of the handsome man that I married. He was cruel and abusive emotionally, spiritually and physically. I will demonstrate events to make this statement clear.

But first I want to take you to the Philippines briefly. We left on a flight without the children each had taken refuge in another place. It didn't take long for me to regret this decision. He was a husband so I guess I should give him a name to make it easier to follow along as I describe the events herein. Let's call him Clyde.

Clyde and I were given a place to live with a family who also looked after us. We arrived just after severe riots when the Marco's; Imelda and her husband were in office. Remember she is the one with all the shoes. We were to get a helicopter into the country in order to reach the providences to the South that was largely untouched by the preaching of the gospel.

So we spent our days talking to officials in order that the helicopter could be brought into the country. We were stationed at the Jimmy Swygert facilities in Manila. The missionary from Europe was with us for a while to set us on track for the mission. Clyde was a "piece of work" He blurted out in the presence of high government personnel derogatory remarks against the leadership of the Philippines.

Our guide from Europe warned him that there is not free speech in the Philippines.

We were then left alone to complete the tasks that were assigned. But Clyde mixed it up with a business associate who was not of the same mindset in respect that he was intrigued with the mission of the helicopter but his reasoning was to use it for personal gain. Meaning to impress the females and open an avenue of assimilating female conquests.

What I am saying here is that Clyde spoke and pretended to be a Christian. I saw in the spirit a picture that represented the essence of what his spiritual person really looked like.

"I saw a person that had and extremely extended stomach. The legs were very thin like they should not have been able to hold up the giant protruding pouch.

I pondered this picture for months until I saw a picture in a book that looked just like the one in my mind. The article described a medical condition that caused this large stomach and small legs because the nutrients were not able to process correctly. This described what I knew in the spirit. Clyde was taking in Spiritual nutrients but rather than processing them correctly in order that he could grow into a healthy Christian he was not allowing the nutrients to process through his spiritual being. And each time this happened it caused his condition to become worse until his spiritual condition was deformed.

I will tell one more incident of the Philippines mostly because the experience was so painful that it is locked from my mind. I started a period and the blood began to pour out like a waterfall. It scared me and I was weak and dizzy. Clyde would not take care of me until the next day so I had to survive for the night thinking that I may did at any minute. The next day he took me to the hospital with the help of our guide. They got the bleeding stopped and I survived. But this describes why I felt vulnerable and extremely unsafe. I felt that I could disappear in a foreign country and Clyde would not be concerned.

This is how I escaped from this ill fated mission. I was extremely careful to say only what Clyde wanted to hear and not let him know what my real plans were. I was desperate to escape the country and reach the safety of home. We had filed a form with authorities that only allowed us to leave the country within three months without filling a tax account. So I needed to act fast. But there was nothing I could do. So guess what? God did something!

He moved upon a friend and fellow teacher in the Christian School from where we departed to write me a letter. In that letter she described the favor that I had with the congregation and leadership.

Imagine that God had set up Clyde to be defeated by his own greed and agenda. He had been making plans to use the helicopter is diverse ways that I mentioned earlier and he wanted a way to get more money. He came up with the plan to send me back to the States to plead with the church to support us in this mission. (He thought it was his idea but it was really his own self centered personality working against him)

I held my breath until I entered the aircraft that would carry me home. My greatest fear happened at the last moment I was ushered to a line to prove that it had not been three months yet and that I did not have to declare taxes. God had mercy and they quickly cleared the matter and I entered the plane. As we waited for take off I began to hyperventilate.

When I arrived home I cancelled all plans to raise money for the mission and I determined that for me this mission was over. Unfortunately it would be another year and a half before the marriage was over.

Here are the three examples of abuses that I promised to relate:

Physical: This is only one incident there were many. Clyde and I walked into our apartment this being after the Philippines and my youngest daughter was living with us. She had not done something while we were gone and he was angry. I was lying on the bed stomach down and back exposed when he took his fist and slammed into my back so hard that I rolled for several minutes trying to regain my breath. I went to the phone and called the police. I got a restraining order that protected both me and my daughter. But we did not make a complete departure for some time yet.

Spiritual: Clyde and I were in our truck and we decided to pray together. He released the words that he wanted God to hear and after he stopped I proceeded to do my part. I began by praying in tongues which was my usual mode of operation. I only had my mouth moving a moment before he told me to "SHUT UP. " I just sat frozen in place and went into the cloudy retreat in my being.

It would be later while in a counseling session that this event was reopened. The perfect moment came for me to reveal it's essence in the presence of our pastor. After I spoke the words that described the assault on tongues (gift of the Holy Spirit) a dreadful silence fell on the conversation No one spoke I moved away fro the two Clyde and our pastor still no sound. The next thing that eventually happened was not a sound but movements to separate exits.

Emotional: Please take the previous explanation of an event in the Philippines that I described for the example of emotional abuse. The one I am referring to is the time that Clyde would not secure necessary medical help and caused me extreme stress.

The last straw was when my daughter and I walked the streets after being locked out of our apartment and running for safety. That was the end. We were divorced after two and a half years.

Clyde shared a dream while we were together. I felt that it had significant meaning but I never shared my interpretation with him because I knew it would be futile to do so. Here is that dream: He said, "I was flying my helicopter with others aboard when the aircraft became out of control and crashed. I was looking down on the crash site and saw devastation and dead bodies. I believed that I was one those who were 'saved' from the crash. Then I looked again and say myself as a dead person among the 'lost.'"

Proverbs 28:18 "Whoso walketh uprightly shall be *saved*, but he that is perverse in his ways shall fall at once."

Psalms 119:176 "I have gone astray like a *lost* sheep: seek thy servant, for I do not forget thy commandments."

6. I GO TO THE STREETS

This chapter is pivotal in respect that if it had not happened the rest of the story would not have as well. The reason being is that we begin with chains being removed from my spirit. I had requested from God that I "Really be a Child of God." Therefore I suppose I needed training that goes the extra mile. As it turns out I clocked a large number of miles over the years. This new venture in my Christian walk began when an awesome older gentleman visited the singles group and explained what he and his sons were doing on Friday nights. When I think of him it is with great respect and admiration. Even though he died a few years after the events that I am about to describe and his family life here turned out to be extra stressful I know he paid a price and he is now benefiting in heaven.

Now without further ado let me explain about the "chains." After this fine gentleman spoke to our group I wanted desperately to join them in the streets where the greatest crime was occurring but there was a struggle going on within. My spiritual eyes were opened and I saw a picture. I saw myself and there were chains tied around my feet and I could not move. I prayed about this vision and I busted through the resistance and I found my self in the streets. I now know that the church at large is in this kind of bondage they do not move into the outer areas away from the church building.

From then on I spent every Friday night in the middle of town with a cloud of witnesses and the residence of the area mostly what is known as street walkers (prostitutes). I still joke that I was a street walker on Van Street (a factitious name) but when the real name is mentioned those who reside in this city know exactly what I am saying.

I approached those with whom I came into contact and spoke to them about Jesus. I spoke a simple message that often led to a precious person asking Jesus to come into their lives and reside as their Savior. The great joy that I received when in the streets set a precedent for my life. From then on I was never satisfied unless I was on the streets sharing with others.

7. IN THE SREETS

There are three memorable incidents that represent the power of God in the streets.

The first that I recall is when I was driving in the car with my husband driving. I saw two women walking on our side of the road. It was dark but still early. I jumped out of the car after requesting that he stop and made my way toward the two women. I walked in their direction until I was within hearing distance and I began verbalizing. I concisely explained the message of Jesus' salvation and asked for a response. They both stared in disbelief until the one said, "I was just taking her to church hoping that she would hear the message of salvation and trust in Jesus as her savior. I was as amazed as she and the lady who was being escorted to church quickly believed after such a confirmation.

There are many precious people that I have spoken to in the streets and they are all equally important. Here is an account of three young men sitting on top of a small mountain. We lived in a town where it was accessible to drive to an area then be able to easily reach the top of the mountain. I found out later that these three young men went to the mountain to search for God. I found this out after their eyes followed me all the way as I left my car and climbed toward them.

I started my anointed presentation geared to speaking the gospel in a simple way when they I stopped because they began telling me why they came to the mountain. They were completely amazed and convinced that God is real and that He heard their pleas to know Him. This was an exceptionally great day with God.

Another time we were witnessing in the park. There were several of us talking to those who would pass by. I looked and two young ladies came into view. I watched until they were near then I approached. I began my simple message of God's plan of salvation when I was interrupted with these words. "I am a Christian and I was on my way with my friend to a photo shoot session for Playboy." She changed her mind after we talked for awhile as she believed it was God who sent me to bring her to her senses.

8. INNER CITY HALF WAY HOUSE

The next step of my evolving into a spiritual giant or wreck, take your pick, they co exist is: An experience in a home for women who were transferring from prison or another trauma and back into society. The women were on one side of the street and the home for the men was right across. My biggest job was keeping the men and the women separated. At least that was my standing joke.

Keeping on track with the theme that pulls these chapters together which is "two forces vying for our lives" brings me to the inner city. I got here because of the people I met while going to the streets witnessing and preaching. My friend from the streets now was the executor of clothing and women's half way house ministry and she invited me to join forces. I accepted and started my duties exhorting our guests, teaching and counseling.

The friend whom I joined worked in conjunction with a church which was also located in the same location with the pastor and associates there in involved. So I was combining with several personalities and level of spiritual growth.

This only incident from this era that I will reveal in this book is one that graphically describes evil and Godly forces in combat.

I was going about my duties one of which involved organizing a Christian band to perform a concert on the inner city grounds in outside earshot of the population. It was around this time that these bazaar events took place.

I accomplished the successful mission event involving the Christian band I just mentioned and during a prayer meeting shortly after this happened:

We were standing in a circle and the co-pastor issued a strong supposedly prophetic word. He spoke of a Jezebel spirit and it was scary and derogative. I immediately suspected that the UN godly word was aimed at me and I wondered, "What the heck is going on here?" The pastor spoke next and he dispelled the word as not being a "Word from God." "Wow this is interesting" I thought.

But the spirits were not finished. I went to Sunday morning service and took my place at the alter to help with ministry as was my usual stance. I approached a girl who was receiving ministry to provide back up support and the pastor moved her away from me. I felt strange and wondered only a moment before I knew for sure.

The pastor moved toward me and called for all the "elders" to encircle me. All of this was done not at my request. I still did not fully understand and I braced myself to hear from God by becoming quiet to receive the ministry.

Than I heard the words that were being said I kept listening not able to emotionally believe these horrible accusations. They were casting out all kinds of demons. It was long ago and I do not remember the details just the pain. After listening and at the time when I was ready I slowly stood and removed myself while they were still speaking. I softly spoke to a person sitting in the seats as I exited. The pastor followed and tried to converse but I only responded with formalities.

I had the opportunity before I left for good to be in a session with the pastor and others in regards to these accusations.

He accused me of somehow acting in a demonic way. Here was his proof. He had a photograph with a faint impression that he said was me. The photograph was taken in the sanctuary and the person supposedly that held the mysterious spot in the photo was demonic.

Here is what really happened: I was walking the grounds as per usual there was plenty to do. We had a clothing and food ministry etc. etc. I was walking past the sanctuary and I thought that I saw some movement. This was the inner city and we were always on guard. I just stuck my face to the window and saw that there was an event going on. So I quickly withdrew not wanting to intrude. This is the proof that he had that enabled him to state that I was a demonic entity.

9. THE FALSE PROPHET

It was a nice afternoon when Ellie and I joined to pray. She and I developed a strong connection and we loved to drive or walk and pray. Ellie considers herself to be a prophet. She has sent prophetic messages to pastors and others.

She married a man several years ago after he went on a mission overseas and the fruit of his ministry confirmed that his prophetic anointing was genuine.

Since they married he has never fulfilled the visions that were and / or are in his heart. I have heard her several times discrediting his ministry and acting as if she wants to stop him from pursuing his dreams.

I at the leading of the Holy Spirit set up a meeting for both of them to meet with a pastor at a critical time. She resisted and convinced seemingly convinced that my project was not a genuine leading of the Holy Spirit. So she called and cancelled for both of them. He did call after she put the brakes on this meeting and said that he wanted to participate. However, by then I had restaged the meeting in another direction.

She had managed to keep him in her control living his life according what she thinks is the current Word from God. Since that time I have not seen them often so I do not know how many times she has sabotaged his ministry. I do know that after more than ten years together he has not been activated for ministry even though it is still strong in his heart.

The meeting that I tried to set up would have brought this husband and a pastor together. It would have been the day after the first election that brought Mr. Clinton to office. I did not know what the outcome of that election would be but God told me that the nation would chose death. (Abortion) The powerful ministry that he would have developed is an administrator of prophetic, strategic and persistent prayer for the duration of that liberal leadership in our nation.

Because his wife cancelled their involvement at the scheduled meeting I rescheduled for another city in which I was the leader. And from there I have had a powerful prophetic ministry to the nations.

Ellie was praying with a friend and I came to know somewhat of their prayer strategy. This person earned her living as a musician. Apparently she was certain that God told her that she would marry a married man in the group. She and Ellie were praying that this man would divorce his wife so he could be free to re-marry. I caught wind of this and challenged them. I was in a living room containing the three of us. My reaction toward their choice of prayer matter completely destroyed any hopes of their prayer being Holy Spirit directed. They however, were convinced that God had told them to pray in this manner. After ten years their prayers were never answered. I was never invited again. Imagine that.

More than ten years ago Ellie believed that God told her to pray that her mother–in–law would die. I guess that was not a genuine prophetic word either as her mother –in-law is still very much alive. This lady is what you can call a false prophet. Stay away from her. I have tried to redirect her but she is steadfastly declaring that she is the one who is right and at least her husband and I are not.

Again after this ten year separation I met Ellie quite by (not an accident) when I was working in a Home Depot Store. I was excited to see her and the past melted away. We met for a prayer session at her home. As we prayed I saw a strong image that was more three dimensional rather than a picture. First I need to mention that we were praying concerning the up-coming national election between then President George W. bush and John Kerry.

As I was walking and praying in my spirit I saw one fire ball larger than the moon coming from outer space. It plunged into the earth even though I did not see the impact I only saw it going past in my peripheral vision to my right. Then in immediate succession two more fiery balls followed. So there were three. I knew at that point that the election results were a done deal in the current president's favor. My proclamation to Ellie that confirmed this victory was met with unbelief. She assured me that there needed to be more prayer or the election results were not assured. I reminded her that she had told me that she sees the "glass half empty." She told me that she was highly offended at my remark and left my presence never to return.

The balls of fire represented the three pre-election debates in which these two men participated.

Trust me on this one if you are a genuine Biblical prophet you have been offended a zillion times.

10. SENTENCED TO TWENTY YEARS IN PRISON?

This is a case for the books. The lady who stars in this portion of the book is what you call "strong willed." I enjoyed her company because she had big plans and I was intrigued. We had a family connection for awhile because my mother married her grand father; therefore, we saw each other occasionally during the holidays.

Did she go to prison for twenty years? I don't know. I haven't heard. This is the situation that I last understood. She admits to sleeping with the foster male teenage young man that graced her home. She was arrested and for about a year she was toying with the courts. She had an elaborate plan to live on the reservation thus avoiding any prison time. Last I heard that option was not on the table.

Here is what happened. She was espousing her faith for some time and I would hear about it from the relatives. I knew that she was "over the edge" or "out of whack" etc. I hadn't an opportunity to talk with her and I knew if I did she would try to overwhelm me with self justification. I did get my chance; she came to our home to deliver my mother some of her personal belongings. I asked that she stay for a drink of soda and I began my challenge. I stuck to my guns insisting that she was not "in faith" but she was what I call "in presumption" I laid out the reasons why she should take the plea deal to be in prison for one year to avoid serving twenty years. She insisted that it was her strong faith that would prevail. Her mother had hired lawyers but the daughter would not follow their council. She was jeopardizing the finances of her mother who was paying for her defense. In other words it was not just she at risk but also her mother who was in the same boat to reap the financial consequences.

I assured her that God would not over ride the governments of law and justice because He is the ordained of such entities. He will not go against Himself. And that she should count herself blessed with only a year to serve.

I do not know the outcome. If someone reads this book and they know these results please contact me.

Texas 1997
Category 5 tornado splits and moves around town.

I lived in Arizona at the time and while sleeping I had a disturbing, to say the least, dream. I saw myself in the place that I lived as a child. I was standing on the edge of the near by town, facing toward my home. At that spot on the horizon, the distance to our house, was approximately a mile. I saw that the sky was black covering the whole area. I thought, "This is not good my son is home alone." It only took a split second before I heard the words, "Your son is dead!" I bolted from my sleep, sitting straight up in bed, instantly declaring loudly, "NO!" I trembled with real feelings, of how I would feel, if one of my sons were to die. It was later, after visiting my family in Texas, that I heard the story. A category five tornado was headed down a straight path, toward the village, where my son and his family live. At that particular time, my son was home alone. As it approached the small town, it split into two tornados and went around, reconnecting on the other side. The tornado continued to the next town causing death and destruction.

11. I HAD A DREAM

For years, many years, at least thirty years I have had a reoccurring dream. Because I am writing this book and I have had to revisit with my mind and emotions the traumas of past marriage type relationships I am reminded of these night visions.

This dream is always about "my man". You know him from the first chapter. In these dreams there is always a variety of strong emotions; ones of wanting, longing, love if you will, and extreme pain of rejection and separation. The environments are always different and each has an individual senero but the emotions and outcome are always the same. I am left with feelings of failure, emptiness and loss.

I am writing now in July 2006 and a couple of nights ago these dreams took such an unusual turn that I have not been able to get it out of my mind.

This dream was completely different. I will try to describe the dream but mostly I am left with the emotions. This time the actions were ones of harmony, acceptance, safety and security. I was with 'my man' and this time when we were together and I knew that the outcome was one of a life long commitment of love and support. When I woke I was disappointed that it had been a dream. But the feelings have stuck. They are now implanted deep within.

12. FROM THE PAST (1993-1995)

In the next few pages you will be reading actual prayer notes from the dates listed. Keep in mind that the theme of this book is spiritual forces fighting for the souls of men as you encounter the following writings. Some of the entries are from a newsletter during the years herein described rather than notes.

13. NORTH KOREA (12-07-1993)

I saw this vision: North Korea was dug up by the root. I did not see any hands digging then I saw it rise from the ground taking with it a perturbing root underneath. Then I saw it being presented to God. It was high above the earth. I saw the large root that was sticking out under the country being cut off. It was cut close to the quick so to speak.

Back on earth where the hole was that was left by the country and root saw a work being done putting in fresh soil. I then saw the country placed back on the ground in the fresh soil. There were new roots beginning to grow and they adapted nicely and began to push their way into the soil. (The large root that was cut off was centrally located under the country. The new little roots that began to grow were placed inside the country but close to the borders all around the exterior.

October 15, 2006 Picture resembles vision of years ago. The country rose up but without hands. There was a root that would be cut off at the top.

Then I heard a loud and clear word "NEW GOVERNMENT." It was incredible different. It was an all new government spiritually as well as political.

14. LITTLE FEET (12-07-1993)

Notes from prayer meeting: While in prayer with a group I began to see feet. I heard God saying, "Come on little feet." I saw the feet begin to stir and twist from side to side as if looking for direction. The Holy Spirit kept saying, "Come on little feet."

Then I wondered if the feet were children's feet because I had received a word about children's feet. I wondered then if it meant literal children or spiritual children.

Then I heard, "Army of children like David." I saw the enemy not only being defeated badly but humiliated also because he was overpowered by such an un-intimidating looking foe.

DAVID vs. GOLIATH THEN SAUL

THERE IS A CHURCH SO MIGHTY AND STRONG,

THEY LIVE AND WORK ALL THE DAY LONG.

BUT MY MIGHTY MEN ARE FEW,

AS FOR THOSE I HAVE, HERE IS A CLUE.

THEY WILL PROSPER IN THEIR NEW LAND,

WHILE THOSE WHO HINDER THEM WILL NOT STAND.

SO THOSE WHO ARE CALLED BY MY NAME,

MUST BEAR FRUIT OR BE REMOVED FROM THE GAME.

FOREVER FREAKS
A band formed by preteen girls:
Laci Ashe-Electric / Acoustic Guitar
Hannah LeGassey-Singer
Maria Garcia-Bass
Kellie Welch (Maby)-Drummer

Forever Freaks for God
Written by: Hannah LeGassey & Laci Ashe

Verse 1
Every one listen up, I'm not even bothering to say "What's up."
Everyone stay, I've got to say, that God is the right way.
When you get on the right ship, it will be worship.
God is the right way, that's what we always say.

Chorus
We are forever freaks for God, we are for God.
Get up, stand up, worship around and fall on the ground,
..........Everybody.......
Get up, stand up, worship around and fall on the ground.
That's all we do, and it's all for you,
We are forever freaks for God.

Verse 2
God is good to us in Him we always trust.
We go ahead and listen; we go ahead and glisten for God.
God is the right way, just as I said the other day.
Go ahead and listen long to this song.

15. PREGNANT WOMAN (05-24-1994)

A vision "A pregnant woman who was way over due was looking for a place to give birth."

(07-29-2006) I Barbara J. Gunsolley the author of this book have something that I would like to add here. I am also the author of "THE VACUUM CLEANER REVELATION" & "WHERE THE HECK ARE THE ROESES." I call them twins and I just gave birth this month July 2006. They have finally gone to press after twelve years of preparation. I do not know if this is the correct or only fulfillment of this prophetic word but I certainly fit the mold of over due.

16. MAGNIFICENT CHARIOTS (03-17-1994)

I don't have words to describe this vision so I am using MAGNIFICENT CHARIOTS. When I originally "saw" these vehicles it was more like I "felt" them. I was in the church sanctuary praying when my spirit opened and I experienced a vehicle that filled the room.

Here are the notes that I recorded concerning this event:

I was praying today about ministries that had large visions but were struggling now. I sensed that they needed a major "breakthrough." I saw methods or vehicles that God could use to "Get things going." God told me that I was coming from a limited perspective. Then I felt a strong presence of God. It was like I was transferred into the heavenly realm. I saw, or felt is more accurate "MAGNIFICENT CHARIOTS." I did not see what they looked like but Ezekiel's Chariot came to mind and I knew they were far above ant transportation I could imagine.

Prayer notes 05-24-1994

A man whom I assumed to be Jesus had a shovel and He was standing on land. He took a few digs with the shovel then He stood still and an edifice just rose up. It went up on this land and the building was transparent and I saw the words "HARVEST HOUSE."

17. AWAKENING

Prepare for the awakening around the earth. There is not enough room to contain for those who are prepared. Are you doing your part to prepare for the awakening? Many are not prepared, not praying, scoffing at and turning their backs on God. He will turn His back on them. They are living in the land of the walking dead.

There is coming an awakening. They shall see and experience mighty things. Put your hand to the plow help others understand spiritual realities. It is easy to fall into temporal realms. What about you? Are you looking to: temporal or the eternal?

It will be even as my prophets have spoken. The tide is coming and it shall flood the land. Take seriously the things of God, the Kingdom of God. Take very seriously the ministry of The Holy Spirit and assignments and positions given in the church.

It is going to happen. You will see the miracle if you can only believe if you are prepared.

Cry out and shed tears and your hearts desire will be given to you. Power dwells within do not give up stand as a watchman. It shall happen you shall see these things.

God is looking for a people who are prepared. This is not a time to eat and drink but to seek hard after the ways of righteousness. Seek with all of your heart and soul. The Kingdom of God and the Word of the Holy Spirit says we are able to do exceedingly more abundantly then we can do or think. The power is within. Look at the frivolous talk in the church. What is God able to do? The mass populations in the Body of Christ have an understanding of God that relegates His power to performing small petitions. Where is the God who parted the Red Sea? He is still the same today, yesterday and forever.

18. PRAYER JOURNEY (07-13-1994)

It was July 13, 1994 and I was about to embark upon a prayer journey which began in the tower above the office. The scriptures of Haggai 1&2 became activated in my spirit and propelled me to pray in agreement with the words spoken by the prophet of old.

"Build the house and I will take pleasure in it...."These words energized the momentum that was beginning to build and I prayed for the house that God was erecting here at our church. And I added prayer the vision residing here in to reach Indochina with the gospel.

I called for the remnant to come and work in this house which was according to the sentence that I was reading and I travailed for people to respond to a strong voice of God that I sensed was saying, "Be obedient and pray."

I continued through the scriptures until I arrived at the address marked Haggai 2:4 at which place I stopped to pray for awhile. "Be strong all you people and work for I Am with you...."This was a firm confirmation that I was on the right road so I moved on.

I was now deep into the verses by now and the fervency of the prayer was increasing in compliance with the words that lead me to shake the nations and lose their silver and gold for the building of the later house which is far more glorious than the former.

The struggle of the scriptures peaked at the point where I saw the *glory of this house and the power of Jesus* over throwing thrones of this world.

When I was nearing the end of chapter 2 the words "I have made you a signet...." jumped off the page and I knew my journey had ended in victory because "signet" meant "authority."

19. A PLACE OF ANTICIPATION (SEPTEMBER-1994)

I am trying to express something inside that defies words so I am calling it *Christmas.*

It is a feeling of great expectancy that I associate with the days and hours when I was a child just before the unwrapping of bright shinny objects that previously resided in the store but now they were under my Christmas tree.

As an adult I have come to know a place of anticipation that surpasses the limitations of my childhood. It is in the silence before a Holy God during times of prayer that I see Him distributing gifts that will not lose their glitter.

The silence is a place of sensing and knowing the person and the power of the Lord, a quiet, peaceful, waiting place of gentle resolve, understanding, listening and communicating.

In this place I gather and build strength just because I am in His presence. And therefore, I am able to stand boldly before Him.

A resolve of conflict in my soul is attained and all the nervousness, apprehension and impatience disappear because in the presence of the Holy Spirit when He sooths me with the oil of this precious gift, *the possessing of my soul*, a suburb victory because this is one of the strongest traits of man.

Now I am able to see and communicate with God and He is able to open up greater realities and reveal Himself more fully.

The exhilaration that I experience in the silence before God causes the juvenile feelings of my past to fade in comparison to the brilliance of the visions and desires that God has for all of His children.

20. A VOLCANO ERUPTS (06-1994)

In a vision the ground began to tremble as the Holy Spirit like a volcano was beginning to erupt. There was a large explosion of power and the fire of God ran in hot torrents like lava toughing, challenging and enveloping all in its path! The news of miracles blew like volcanic ash across the land by the wind of God.

In another vision a large explosion was seen over dry land in the form of a powerful thunderstorm. Blessings poured out from this powerful storm like rivers of water (the Holy Spirit), flooding accompanied with lightning (God's presence) and thunder (God's voice).

There was a vision of darkness and grieving for the Body of Christ, especially in the area of unity. Repentance and a willingness to look at truth seemed to be the aim of God to eliminate the hindrances to His plans. *Ezekiel 3*

21. I SAW GOD SITTING ON A THRONE (06-28-1994)

I saw God sitting on a throne. He was dressed in a white robe. Our prayers were petitioning Him and He was looking down at the petitioner who was praying in the spirit. There were people coming down stairs on either side of the throne and every one of the sides was listening to a revelation in intercession.

There was an intense battle today and rooting out with something like a long knife. It was easily cutting through the roots although it was a lot of work. The prayer was so powerful. Two roots were pulled down from the high places. It was a new level of prayer. Deep roots of evil were destroyed and each slice of the knife was a perfect hit. We kept pulling the roots out.

(06-30-1994) Knocking on the door and seeking hard after the Kingdom of God for the nations. There were deliverances and freedom for the nations of Indo china and India. There was a great light coming from the North. There were deliverance and freedom for the nations of Indo China. It sees it! An army ready to go. Provisions available and they are ready to go. All kinds of provisions as soon the door opens they are ready to go. I see the darkness opening up. A door is opening now and the army is ready to go. Like when the Iron Curtin came down and the army of God flooded the nations.

We are a fully equipped army as we pray and receive these provisions from the Holy Spirit. We are going after greater spiritual opposition which will give us greater victories. This is not more difficult that going after lesser strongholds if we are properly equipped.

I see a mighty opening into the 10/40 window (middle and far eastern nations) Awakening like a veil coming off. There is a mighty opening for the gospel. They can now hear because the veil has been ripped off. It's time to go in with the gospel. Your people are ready and prepared to go. (It was somewhere close to this time that TRINITY BROADCASTING opened stations is this area.)

22. RECORDING THE VISION (06-30-1994)

After evening leadership training class Pastor mentioned a verse in Habakkuk 2:2 *Then the Lord answered me and said, "Write the vision in plain on tablets, that he may run who reads it."* Well this morning on the way into work the Lord said pray for the prosperity for the saints. So when I entered the prayer room that is what I did. Then as I was praying the Holy Spirit showed me the last part of Zephaniah 1; 6 *A day of trumpet and alarm against the fortified cities and the high towers.* Then I saw myself climbing up a tower ladder.

I asked the Lord to show me what was at the top of the tower and I pushed open something like a metal top and looked out to a place filled with gold shinning real brightly. Then the Holy Spirit said to turn the page in my Bible to the end of Zephaniah 3:20 *"… at that time I will bring you back, Even at the time I gather you; for I will give you fame and praise among the peoples of the earth, when I return your captives before your eyes, Says the Lord."* I can't remember when else I ever laughed, cried and drooled all at the same time.

23. INTO THE FUTURE

Now is the time for all good men (women) to come to the aid of their country. Notify, the people of the UNITES STATES OF AMERICA, that this coming presidential election is pivotal and crucial. I have picked this date, 06,26,2006, because this is the time, that I am hearing from the Holy Spirit, to begin the creation of these pages. I do not know the title of this book yet, but I do know the objective: Now, is the strategic timing to produce the best results.

This nation is deeply rooted in prophecy (words from God that will be fulfilled or can be changed based upon repentance). An example is the city of Nineveh which turned and obeyed God as in the story of Jonah in the Bible. The outcome of the next election will determine the result.

Today our great nation is being torn apart by two opposing philosophies. It is black and white in respect to the crucial criteria which is the choice for life or death.

As we travel into the future in these pages is aware of this concept: Abraham Lincoln declared that the slaves were free by speaking and writing the words but it took a war and then some to actually bring it to reality.

As prophets and prayer warriors our job is to declare God's living Word in His timing and then it is His responsibility to bring it into reality. And I assure you that anything that God has spoken will come to pass. Not one of His words will fall to the ground and they will all be fulfilled.

These next pages will explain how to communicate in a way that will touch the heart of God and cause that His blessings will remain on our nation. And that we as a Godly nation can continue to be an influence for freedom and righteousness to the nations on the earth.

24. DISCIPLINED ANGER

What the heck is that? We as Christians are paranoid when the word anger is spoken within a text of any sort. The general response when this word is said is one of resistance because there is a deep rooted belief that if you are angry sin must be involved and repentance is needed.

Lighten up! If you never get angry how are you going to deal with demonic assaults on yourselves and your families etc?

Getting angry with the devil is a healthy way to deal with pain and suffering rather than just stuffing your feelings and *doing the good Christian thing, forgiving.*

I do not forgive the devil and DARN IT! STOP confusing your feelings for people with those of your real enemy, demonic forces. God assures in His word that they do very much exist and you may hate them with mucho gusto.

The slogan that I wrote to express the aim of a prayer ministry in the 1980's is; DESTROYING THE WORKS OF THE DEVIL THROUGH DISCIPLINED ANGER: *PRAYER*

A good way to combat depression (internally directed anger) is to get mad at the real source and fight. Pick up your sword, the Word of God and kick the crap out of your enemy.

Oh yes! Real feelings, real anger, real victories, real combat, not fake ritual that resembles prayer.

25. CONFRONTING EVIL FORCES IN HIGH PLACES

Confronting evil forces in high places is not something that you would do without specific guidance and leading of the Holy Spirit.

First I want to identify some of these evil forces through the next words that I will write. The devil and his armies of demons have managed to convince a large section of mainline Christianity that the gifts of the Holy Spirit were meant for the original days of Christianity and not for today. These gifts such as; speaking in tongues, interpretation of tongues, prophecy, healings, words of wisdom, and words of knowledge that were poured out on Pentecost shortly after the death of Christ and which were meant to be weapons against the demonic have been banned from some churches. Therefore they are ill equipped for the day in which we live.

There are those who have gained in strength to keep in step and who have the weapons to deal with the spiritual forces on the earth; but there are only a few. As for those who have refused to change they are not equipped to function as a formidable foe in today's society i.e. THE LAST DAYS.

The occult has infiltrated the common grounds of our society injecting their spiritual prowess of demonic origin into our culture as a norm. Television programs movies and books draw people into a belief system that once you are caught in its jaws they close like an iron trap. Children are vulnerable as they are just beginning to learn about their surroundings and they are brainwashed quickly.

The powers of the demonic have gained in great strength. The flood gates of sexual perversion are flooding our nation. The strength of the onslaught of pornographic stimuli is so pervasive that unless you have been vaccinated by God you are drowning in the disease.

This is only a brief view of a global spiritual holocaust. What I am doing in the next chapters is offering information that will help get those who are interested into a place of spirituality that is able to handle our current situation. Keeping in mind that as time progresses it's the responsibility of those who want to keep in step with the moving of God to do so; as things will continue to change. And today's information will soon be outdated.

26. THE SPIRITUAL GIFTS ARE NEEDED BECAUSE?

If you are asking why is it so important that the gifts of the Holy Spirit be activated in our lives it is because this is the avenue that God has chosen to communicate with His people?

The kind of prayer needed in these days is what I call prayer in the spirit as opposed to flesh prayer.

And while I am mentioning prayer let me explain that it is praying in agreement with the Holy Spirit that is the position of victory for those who are succeeding in these demonic influenced days.

If you are praying in the flesh as do most people it is of your own understanding and it goes something like this: After presenting your prayer requests you bow your heads and begin to re- speak everything that had just been said, as if God could not hear, and/or He was not present, and/or He is too stupid to get it the first time, and/or.....You get the picture. This is flesh prayer because if you were in the spirit you would know that God was in the room because He is spirit and so are you.

I just read an article in the paper this morning in the community where I live. There is an article asking that people come together at a specific location and pray for the unborn. I am not concerned if these prayers are in the flesh or spirit the effort will please God and He will receive their prayers. I just wanted to put this paragraph here to bring a balance to my writing as is what God always does.

Those who worship Him (or pray) must do so in *spirit and truth*.

Therefore, the gifts of which I am speak found in 1ˢᵗ Corinthians 12 describe avenues in which we are able through the spiritual realm to hear from God and to release the words that we hear. When these words are released and the fruit of the ministry is confirmed (your word was correct and it went right to the source that God was targeting) you and the Holy Spirit form a team that transpires the earthly realm and achieves victories in the spirit that will last forever and will not return void.

Let's examine these gifts in Corinthians. The word of wisdom, the word of knowledge, faith, gifts of healings, working of miracles, prophecy, discerning of spirits, different kinds of tongues and interpretation of tongues. Anyone who is functioning in any of these gifts is closely connected to the Holy Spirit. The manifestations of these gifts only happen when a genuine anointing comes from God upon the person who is administering the gift. This is why I am saying that anywhere the spiritual gifts are not manifesting, for what ever reason, there cannot be victories to the extent needed in the world as it is today because it is only flesh ministry. There needs to be a partnership with the Holy Spirit.

And to move it up another notch the ministry of in the spirit needs to be matured in order to be successful. Those who are being called now to the front lines have been ministering in their spirit with the Holy Spirit for some time. And they have been tested and gone through the fires and have come out as pure gold. Those who have not paid the price will not be brought forth now. But if you are willing to go back into the fire and be tested your time will come.

27. KEEP IN MIND WHERE I AM GOING WITH THIS

Keep in mind where I am going with this (spiritual gifts). It is to the high places in prayer to combat large demonic strongholds over the entire earth. With that in mind let me proceed. Not everyone is called to this ministry but God is instigating the writing of this book so He is doing something. I am presuming at this point that he is rising up an army for such a time as this to move in a powerful anointing to tear down strongholds across the world for the purpose of furthering the gospel to be preached in the entire world.

Therefore, what I am saying is that when this army is functioning they are firmly connected with the Holy Spirit and it is from this perspective that the victories are able to be achieved. And it is the only way to succeed.

When I was a young Christian my pastor, whom I loved dearly and who is now deiced (Pastor Green in Scottsdale AZ. Peoples Church in the 1970's and 1980's) spoke many times of the great, elderly, women saints who were prayer warriors. At that time I felt like we as women were being patronized. Now I understand that he knew something that I was yet to learn.

Times are a changing. In the olden days, which ever period you pick, there was not the extent of activities and connectedness that exists today. Therefore now is a specific time with a specific challenge. Those who flow in this move of God will be doing so from the high places.

So I guess I need to explain to the best of my ability what the heck are the *high places?*

There are principalities and powers and spiritual wickedness in high places. There are levels of authorities over the earth such as:

Demonic rulers who stress to keep control over large areas and who have devils of lesser rank under them. These strongholds are not mapped as per square miles. The areas of control and bondage are designed to such headings as; False Religions, sexual perversions, lies and deception, greed and power, selfishness and self indulgence, etc. These places of demonic activity manifest as. Religions whose founders built their faiths on a false word from supposedly god and have subsequently enslaved millions of people. I would not want to be one of these founding fathers on judgment day if they did not repent before their deaths.

You get the idea. The money of the nations is either being used to further righteousness and truth or it is supporting lies. So the major stronghold that spiritual entities are fighting to control is the wealth of the world because it is power to further what ever is the goal. God declares that all the gold is His. It is just a matter of His saints taking possession of it for the promotion of righteousness on the earth.

If you would take a minute and visit the Bible from front to back you will find that God wins. However, He has chosen to work through His people. So get in line, take your place, pick up your weapon and wait for your orders then fight.

28. PROVIDE FINANCES FOR PRAYER

Traditionally those who pray are in the back rooms of the churches and do not receive a salary as they are volunteers. I do not know anyone who gets paid to pray. Although I imagine that it does happen.

Because the ministry of Prophetic Prayer is intricately involved in end time ministry there needs to be a budget to support this vital section of the army. Therefore, the goal for my book (THE VACUUM CLEANER REVELATION) which has gone to press as of July 2006 is to financially support prophetic prayer ministries.

All of a sudden I am using the term *prophetic prayer.* You already know what kind of prayer this is if you have read the previous chapters. It is simply prayer that is in agreement with God's Word and the leading of the Holy Spirit. And once this prayer comes forth it cannot return void because it is a living Word of God. That is why it is called prophetic because true prophecy is always fulfilled.

This is the prayer that changes the face of the globe to set the captives free that they may know and worship the living and true God of the Bible.

Today is August 5, 2006 and I am typing this chapter of my; as yet un-titled next book. THE VACUUM CLEANER REVELATION went to press July 2006. I am in my bedroom/office and truthfully even though I know the finances will come and the goal will be met, as a person walking out this vision daily I feel so far away from the reality of the fulfilling of this dream.

I long for my room to be filled with those who love to enter the presence of God and pray. I desperately want to give precious prayer warriors who are also vulnerable and loving family and community member's money for their vital service.

29. REAL FEELINGS TODAY

Today I am beginning the training portion of this book Today I feel defeated. I feel like I have worked so hard getting three books to press because I felt that God was leading me. I know that what I have been doing has been totally confirmed by the Holy Spirit every step of the way.

But yesterday I had to fight again. An important paragraph from my last book was removed after I approved the galley. This was a definite attack upon the book it happened because a person deleted the words there is no other way that it could have happened. The problem is not with the person, it may have been a mistake, and it is with the demonic realm. This person either deliberately sabotages the manuscript because of his/her extreme opposition to the message or he/she was just a pawn who made a mistake.

I looked at the sales of my first book today it has been on the market for a few weeks. There is only one sale and that was my mom. This made me feel rejected and defeated. I have not worked at a full time secular job since I began the production of these books back in February of 2006. I had money to carry me through but the demonic realm caused so many delays and I had to fight hard to regain my ground. I had a couple of part time jobs that did not work out. My finances have run out and I am living on credit. I cannot do this much longer. Every day I wake with pain in my gut because of the lack of funds but it goes away after I get started working. I am now struggling with continuing or getting a job. If I did it would take me away from my tasks and because of the constant struggle to overcome opposition to these goals I cannot leave my babies unprotected. I am in a dilemma will I go on and trust God and take care of my books until they are prospering on their own or will I spend my time making money so I won't lose my good credit etc.

My family has come around somewhat after seeing the results of what I have accomplished so far. My websites are professional etc. But I sense and hear the doubts that I can succeed which come from those who love me and want to protect me from myself.

I have waited since 1999 to again be used of God. I feel that now is my time and I declare that this is so. Today I feel defeated. Tomorrow I will see the miraculous intervention of God.

30. PROPHETIC PRAYER TRAINING

These next chapters are the most important of this book. They are instructions on how to win the favor of God and genuinely expect that He is moving on behalf of your requests. Not only is he answering your prayers He is actually a partner in the instigation of the responses.

Job requirements:

1. In order to achieve the objectives of causing changes in the "HIGH PLACES" We must be tightly entwined within the goals and visions of God. (As written in The Bible)

2. To be successful you will pay a price. You will keep going no matter what circumstances seemingly appear because our advisory uses mind games as a weapon.

3. The rewards of being in the presence of the Holy Spirit at any given moment far out way the negative aspects of ministering in prayer.

4. Spiritual growth in essential. No matter where you are in your walk with God you will grow exceedingly.

5. You are called. You know that you hear the voice of God and that He is leading you.

6. You will know how to touch the heart of God through Worship which is the cornerstone of prayer that touches nations.

7. You will have separated yourself from influences of the demonic around you so there will not be an avenue where you can be systematically attacked.

8. You will not be confident in yourselves but you will have learned to rely of The Holy Spirit no matter what the circumstances say.

9. You need not as yet have reached a level of spiritual maturity that you think is necessary. The only requirements is that you are "called"

10. Be prepared to have the most wonderful time of your lives in the presence of God.

31. PRAYING WITH FERVOR

"Committed, proven women of God praying with fervor and Holy Spirit strategy for a spiritual awakening great enough to impact our cities like a bomb."

This statement was written in the 1990's as a goal in my prayer ministry. Our objective was and is to bring an explosive change to cause deliverances for those who are captives of evil spiritual bondages.

In the spiritual realm these goals are very attainable and they then manifest into the natural realm. There will be a great awakening great enough to impact our cities like a bomb. To combat God's objective to set captives free the demonic the demonic is also using bombs. But they can only manifest their bombs in the natural realm so they send suicide bombers.

These combustible type events are evidenced in the 2001attack on the World Trade Center. There is always a connection between what is happening in the spiritual and in the natural because it first happens in the spirit then it manifests in the natural realm.

God spoke; then the world was created. The spiritual is the spoken living Word of God that is "anointed" for a specific mission. The natural is where we walk and talk on a daily basis, touching feeling and seeing etc.

The devil, however, does not have the advantage of spiritual weapons. He cannot speak and cause things to happen. He needs to rely of using his low level demons who are wimps. He uses deception and lies etc to achieve his objective which is to control the earth. Satan lost his authority upon the earth spiritually when Jesus died. We are now walking out the process of taking the control of the earth away from the devil into the natural realm. Satan knows his days are numbered and he is just grasping onto a last hurrah.

Therefore, as a prayer general I anticipate that strategic bombs are poised and waiting for instructions to be released and detonated onto demonic forces.

32. SEE INTO THE SPIRITUAL REALM

We as residents of this earth are trained and habitually understand boundaries such as: Where our home is located? What city do we live in? Who or what are the powers that make decisions for us as a community? What country do we live in? What are the odds that we can live a fulfilled life in this country? On the map how far is it to a place of safety if needed?

The spiritual realm is mapped out differently such as: Community organizations that perpetrate a false doctrine or teaching onto people and it affects the outcome of their lives collectively and negatively. The locations of our dwelling places are mapped in categories such as; we are living in truth and freedom or are we living in a place of bondage and entrapment? The city where we live is connected to other spiritual places such as; A community in which we live involves not the physical location but all those who live here have been indoctrinated into something evil (sin or false teaching) and they are being systematically destroyed. I.e. those who are trapped in sexual bondage which destroys healthy relationships that perpetrate the strong bonds of family life for the support of all concerned. Or we live in a spiritual community that is supported based upon Biblical principles and this connection strengthens us as individuals and as members of a network.

The areas in the spirit do not end at the border of a nation. That is why prophetic/strategic prayer works so well. It looks right into the spiritual realm where the intervention needs to occur before it can manifest into the natural. Most prayer is blind sighted because it is reacting to something that has already happened instead of focusing on pre-emptive strikes.

33. FIRST DAY OF NEW PROPHETIC/STRATEGIC PRAYER MEETING

Let's start from the beginning. Today is your first prayer meeting. You have invited several interested women and you have studied and prepared. What is the first thing that you do after greeting and meeting? You all have your heads bowed now what?

The most important and actually the only thing that you need do is: "Invite the Holy Spirit." You each have your own personalities and ways of communicating but I suggest that you not be wimpy about approaching God. Do something that you have not done before. Erase all the people in the room from your mind so that you are not inhibited in your effort to please God.

I stand and move and begin to pace and pray in tongues for awhile waiting on God for the manifesting of His presence. I am honest and tell Him if I am having a bad day then I quickly focus on His presence and power to overcome any negative emotions I may have and He draws me into the realm where He lives and we begin to speak to each other.

I speak loudly as this is my nature and I tell God genuinely of all the great things that He is and what He does. If you think this is bribing God you are right but it really works because He really likes it and I get anything I want. The thing is that what I want is what He wants. I come into agreement with His Word so that I know we want the same things and I am never disappointed in the results.

So now your group has entered a spiritual level where your prayers are not in the flesh. You will have to continue to monitor the sounds in the room and when you hear the prayers regressing into the flesh redirect them again into the spirit.

Flesh prayers are easily recognized they are lifeless and drown on and on. Spirit prayers are quickened by God and you feel like electricity is clicking from one person to the other as they jump in and speak the words that are welling up from within by the anointing of the Holy Spirit.

34. PHYSICAL ENVIRNOMENT FOR PRAYER ROOM

Before your meetings and as you go and grow your prayer room will take on a personality of its own. At the leading of the Holy Spirit you will be placing pictures, maps, newspaper articles, school rosters, names of political leaders, etc within the room for those who are praying to access at the leading of the Holy Spirit. Actual Bibles need to be in the room as well as scriptures written on cards. All of this kind of stimuli can lead the group to a successful encounter with opposing forces. God will direct and it helps to be able to move freely without having to stop and do research.

It is important to have a voice recorder in the room because you will want the information. You may not be able to remember everything especially the anointed messages that come forth in the height of an encounter with God. If you were to try to revisit you would not be able to because you are no longer in that place in the spirit.

You need a place to pray where you are not concerned about who will hear. We have had prayer times where we cried uncontrollably and those times when we laughed until we were rolling on the ground.

You can expect unusual manifestations occasionally mostly from exterior sources near your environment. The demonic realm will manifest in a presence where God is strong.

If your goal is for the nations you will need maps all over the walls. It is incredible what God does as you go into the high places in the spirit. Your eyes open up and you are drawn to a place on the map; you begin to pray and prophecy what the Holy Spirit is saying. It is so awesome to be in God's presence nothing else compares.

The way to the high places is through worship of God. He will lift you into the heavenly realm as you please Him through seeking hard after His Kingdom in spirit and in truth.

35. WHAT IS STRATEGIC PRAYER?

Strategic prayer is as the word implies. It is a series of events that need to transpire in order for a goal to be accomplished. There are lots of strategy materials in the Bible.

Here is an example: There was a prayer need for the pastors to get into the new church building that they had been working on for some time. They reported to us that there was a major problem confronting them at the last minute. We are in a prayer a session and during a time before God someone heard that there were three strongholds that needed to be taken care of for the plan to go forward. So we continued in travail looking and seeking for supernatural answers and strategies. They someone opened the Bible where it talks about shooting arrows. (*Psalms 58:7*) It said that God will shoot them (His enemies) with His arrows. So as a strategy we just updated the Bible to the 20th Century and changed the arrows to rockets. We positioned these rockets in prayer to hit each of the three targets that was revealed as the place that needed to surrender to the plan of God for these pastors. (Don't get concerned about the rockets it is the principle that does the work)

The next Sunday the pastor reported that the three hindrances to purchasing the new building came together in agreement and the plan went forth. It was three entities like a finance company, a real estate company and one other. I don't remember exactly it was long ago.

For the nations there is a constant need to continue seeking the will and strategy of God. His will is that all would hear the gospel and be saved so no need to spend any more time on that issue it is settled.

So it is the strategies that we need to be concerned with. Each situation has a unique God ordained system of events that need to happen before those whom He has called from before the foundations of the world can be set free. There are evil principalities and powers on the earth placed here by God because Satan blew it badly in heaven. Now they are our problem but God sent His son so that we can defeat the enemy and in fact he has already lost. We that are here on the earth have the job of joining with the Holy Spirit to use the authority that was purchased by Jesus and given to us. (All power in heaven and earth has been given to Me and I give it to you, says, Jesus. (Place scripture here.) Therefore it is our duty to take control of our planet in prayer and spoil the plans of the devil.

This simple truth that God is present and powerful is almost completely buried in religious observations and rituals. The reality of a dynamic, loving God has manifested but few see the truth. They continue living their lives speaking about politics and religion as if The Holy Spirit was a ghost of history, Can you see God? You have really missed some good stuff. I see Him moving all the time? You see a news report.

36. VISION OF WAVES (05-04-2006)

As I prayed on this date I saw the following picture and I put it on paper: "Waves surrounding the United States of America. The jagged tips of forceful spurts of water were banging against our borders. The waters of waves were positional on all sides even those where in the natural the oceans do not exist. The waters were not blessings but judgment. I sensed that the waves were growing in stature and strength but they were presently being held back by righteous leadership."

2 Samuel 2-7 *And He said: The Lord is my **ROCK** and my fortress and my deliver; The God of my strength, in whom shall I trust; My shield and the horn of my salvation, my stronghold and my refuge; My Savior, You save me from violence. I will call upon the Lord, who is worthy to be praised; so shall I be saved from my enemies. **When the waves of death surround me, the floods of ungodliness make me afraid. The sorrows of Sheol surround me; the snares of death confront me.** In my distress I called upon the Lord, and cried out to my God; He heard my voice from His temple, and my cry entered His ears.*

PROPHETIC WORD FOR THE 2008 PRESIDENTIAL ELECTION: (If you have been a member of a political party forever do not continue now. You, of course, can vote either way but your vote must be based upon this criterion, **("WHAT DOES GOD SAY ABOUT ANY AND ALL OF EVERY ISSUE BROUGHT UP AS A VIABLE INTEREST OF THE NATIONS' VOTERS. YOU MUST WEIGH THE CANDIDATES UPON THE ROCK OR THE ROCK WILL FALL UPON YOU?")** **BARBARA J. GUNSOLLEY**

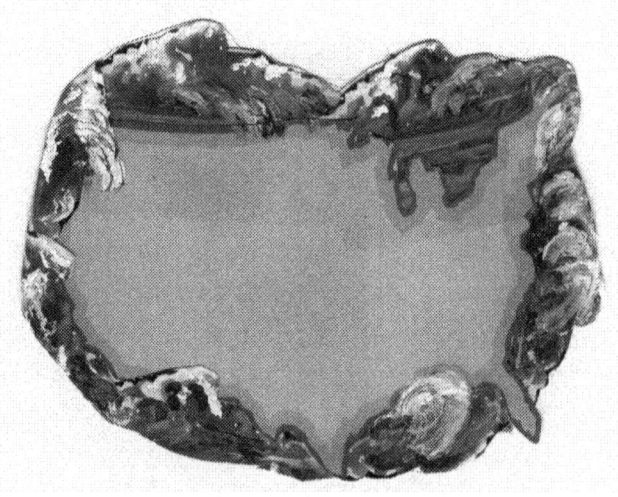

37. GEORGE WSHINGTON'S VISION FOR THE UNITED STATES

In the late 1970's I taught in a Christian school for six years. During that time I was exposed to a book that was being read to the group I was attending. I cannot remember many details but I just searched the internet and there is plenty of evidence to support the fact that our first president, George Washington, had prophetic visions.

There were several prophetic pictures, in the book, that described wars that the new Union would eventually face. Most of the visions are fulfilled. They described the civil war and others. But the prophetic picture, with which, I am most impressed, is the one yet to come.

Here is what I remember and I believe we have entered this phase of prophetic fulfillment. The picture I heard is that of forces, coming, and surrounding the United States on all sides. They came by sea and land. Then fighting broke out in the major cities. It appeared that the United States of America was defeated. Then like in a movie, at the last minute, she rose up in victory.

The prophetic picture from the past describes this new war on terror. The fact that President George W. Bush has taken the war to the terrorists in their territory may avert this picture from fulfillment. But, more likely, the vision will become reality.

The reason that this prophetic picture is so unique is the fact that in the days gone by, great armies came with a full display of power. This vision could only be accomplished today, by secretive entries into our nation, like the September 11, 2001 attack.

If this nation continues to choose righteous leadership, those who standards are Biblical, as did they in the city of Nineveh, where the people at the time, repentance from evil, after hearing Jonah preach, we can be spared this visions' fulfillment. A good start is the elections of George W. Bush for two more terms. There is a great spiritual battle brewing for either the devastation described in the vision or a reprieve brought about by repentance as in the city of Nineveh.

38. PROPHECY LOOMIMG

Now that I inserted a prophecy spoken centuries ago that may be relevant for today let's regroup. Is there something that we can do? There is always a chance that God will relent if the nation makes some good choices. I just read Ezekiel this morning the first chapters and the people of Israel at that time had crossed the line. The time for repentance had passed and judgment was eminent.

I am coming from the perspective that there is still a chance to ward off this prophecy from fulfillment at this time. My job as a prayer warrior is to keep fighting no matter what and that is why I am writing this book.

I am hoping and praying that this book will be read by masses and that because of its contents prophetic prayer groups will fill the nation. And that the prayer will begin, as Soon as possible, because the time is short.

39. HEAVY CLOUDS

I was driving to Home Depot my favorite store when my eyes were drawn to the cloud above me. It was tubular in shape and it stretched from the horizon to over my head. Far away at the beginning of the cloud it was narrow but as it came closer where it covered of my head it gradually became larger. I was struck by the shape and I wondered if God was telling me something. The next day mom and I went to the mall to walk. When we exited the car she looked up and said, "Look at that cloud it feels heavy and oppressive at first I thought it was smoke from a fire." I was amazed that it was the same shape as the one I saw yesterday. I quickly determined that God was indeed speaking.

Clouds of depression and disease have cumulated in proportions of mass amounts because the nations have been on this earth for a long time and they have grown and multiplied. A cloud has formed from centuries of abuses of God's plans and purposes being ignored and distained. The end times are a cumulating of everything that has been done and spoken that has contributed either for the good of the nations by proclaiming truth or by ignoring a righteous God deliberately thus diseases are the results and they are filling the earth. *Ezekiel 3:1-3* **The Word of the Lord came to me again saying, thus says the Lord God: "Wail, Woe to the day!" For the day is near: It will be a day of clouds, the time of the gentiles.**

These diseases are spiritual, physical and mental. Sick thinking that is not based upon the simple Ten Commandments and principles in the Bible cause chaos. When God's rules are in force they provide a safe and productive environment in which to live as nations and peoples.

God has declared that; "This gospel of the Kingdom of God will be preached in the entire world then shall the end come," Therefore there is still time.

I am prophetically stating that the war in Iraq will open the Middle East to democracy for a specific God ordained reason. To bring forth a new era of freedom for those who live in these areas so that they may be free to hear the gospel of Christ.

The air via TV signals proclaim the good news now through Christian Television but God will ensure that the people may be free to hear the good news.

It is imperative that we as a nation here in the Unites States of America as we approach the next presidential election change our ways of thinking.

You must no longer think, "Political party." If you have been a member of a party forever do not continue now. You, of course, may vote either way but your vote must be based upon this criteria: "What does God say about any and all of every issue brought up as a viable interest of the nation's voters. You must weigh the candidates upon the Rock or the Rock will fall upon you.

Now is the time that we as a nation will determine the results. Will the cloud be as my mother stated as her first impression? *Fire of the Holy Spirit* or will the choice of the nation be to again ignore God thus plummeting us into a depression?

40. VOICE CLOUDS

I just finished the writing of the book and spent yesterday working on the front cover. I had the concept in my mind but it changed somewhat as I proceeded because of materials that I did not have and had to get from the store. I bought stick on letters because of the black background. I could not use the computer to print color on black because the colors became black like the background when I printed them out. So I began to spell the title out in letters across the top of the cover and learned that they did not fit. So I began to trying to access a word in my mind that was close to the other but was shorter. I could not find one (Cumulating clouds). I would keep the word clouds but what was the other word? I examined the dictionary looking for a similar word that meant the same thing as cumulating but nothing struck me as being what I wanted. So I re-read some script on the last page looking for a clue and I was hit by the phrase (was God trying to <u>tell me</u> something) so I changed to "Voice Clouds." It was a short word that would fit.

This morning I am still listening to what needs to be done yet to the cover. I looked at the picture and this time I saw clearly black and white combined to make the cloud that graces the cover. Now I am understanding prophetically that the voice cloud is a result of centuries of combining two ways of think that are diametrically opposed and do not combine. Therefore the black and white in the clouds are positioned together but they do not mix that is why there is a combustible situation beginning to andance further because it cannot be contained in the cloud any longer. It is a storm that erupts at a time when the clouds burst and deliver their contents upon the earth. The white is the "Complete truth and power of Words of God as spoken and recorded in the Bible." The black in the cloud represents the anti- Christ message distaining God's Words.

These two forces and mingling will soon erupt into a terrible storm. The fire around the edges represents the Fire of the Holy Spirit that comes forth through people who are following Him and because of their obedience and prayers there is a possibility that this fire will prevail as a mighty move of God which will avert this great storm for now.

LITTLE VOICE I am amazed as I am finishing the last chapters of; "Voice Clouds," that there is an even further significance concerning voices. I am reminded that in the early 1990's when I wrote; "The Vacuum Cleaner Revelation," I was represented within the text as a little voice. I am seeing that because I have now written and released (this being the third) three books, my voice is no longer considered small. "My voice," meaning the words that I have published that are Words from God for today.

This new reality is just now sinking into my spirit and I am realizing that I am a part of the; "Last day prophets," recorded in the last chapter of; "The Vacuum Cleaner Revelation." The words that I have spoken in this book (Voice Clouds) need to be taken seriously.

MOVEMENT OF HIS MIGHT

At a time when you think not…

Everything good and pure that you have sought,

Will emerge from the darkness, as pure light

And cause in My house a fearful sight.

Beyond the limits of trees and flowers,

Your love for the lost supported the hours,

Spent day by day and night by night,

To secure from the Lord a movement of His might!

I saw Jesus standing on land with a shovel in His hands. He drove the tool into the ground twice before standing still. Then an edifice rose from the ground. The building was *TRANSPARENT* and I heard the words; *HARVEST HOUSE*"

Recently as I flipped through the T. V. channels I saw and heard a prolific Biblical preacher declaring that "Transparency" is the current word for the churches. When he spoke my spirit leaped with confirmation. At that time I did not remember that the text of my book contained this word. Since then during the process of waiting for editing to be completed for "Voice Clouds," I remembered that the term "Transparent" was within my book. The confirmation that I heard on T.V dictated that I put this picture on the back cover.

Continuing as per usual for my writing style as I am obviously still in revelation mode and more is being added to this written account. My interpretation of "Transparent," as it relates to the churches for today is; living our lives as real people as we follow the leading of the Holy Spirit being obedient, and making mistakes. Continuing and pressing on with an anointing from God that enables us to accomplish what has been set before us. As a result and because the Holy Spirit is involved we must be open and honest in all our dealings.

An example of transparency in the Bible is; the entire Bible. This book does not contain the most recent and dynamic preaching styles or relevant information gleaned from the scriptures for Sunday sermon.

The most widely read book in the world contains everyday and lifetime events of real people as they walk out there lives in real situations. And because of the interventions of God; their lives declare His glory or reveal defeat at His hand. Thus, the stories therein reveal individuals as they encounter people and events on a small or large scale that will shape the nations and the future of man kind.

I am an individual. I am and have been going about my business daily seeking and including the Holy Spirit in everything that I do.

Thus, I have written three books "Voice Clouds" being the third and in each book are recorded events from life as they happen. And I am careful to give the Holy Spirit His due place in these real stories. What I am saying is that my writing style is the same as that of the Bible. Therefore, as I understand the word "Transparent," it means real life with exposure to successes, failures, and yes sins.

You will read in my books of events in which I was accused of being demonic or containing a demon. In the religious circles this is the most hurtful thing that could happen to a Christian. Because of the culture of Christianity as it now stands the exterior presence portrayed to the congregation are one of selected and pre approved criteria. And one sided because the one in "authority" speaks influencing what the onlookers will believe not allowing another opinion to be spoken. The opportunity to challenge these untouchable leaders is difficult at best.

This stigma of being accused of having a demon is at times perpetrated against precious and completely innocent Christians. And because of this a "Spirit of fear" which is demonic comes upon the person and they are afraid to tell anyone fearing that a seed of doubt about their faithfulness to Jesus will be planted in others as well.

This is where being "Transparent" can be beneficial. If those who minister know that people are not afraid to speak up and be transparent the enemy will lose his grip perpetrated through fear and lies.

As I mentioned I am still waiting for the book, "Voice Clouds" to go to press. It has been since July that the other two books; "The Vacuum Cleaner Revelation" & "Where the Heck is the Roses" have been available for sale. I have diligently worked all the angles that I know to promote these books. One of the methods that I use is to knock on the doors of the churches and ask that I be let in. I designed a web site for them to view and that, with the information within my books provide the credentials needed to be let into the churches to minister.

A Catholic pastor of a charismatic church emailed me and viewed my site. He wrote an encouraging and helpful message. I sent him my books and I have not heard again. That is O.K. at least he responded. I have emailed countless and I mean I don't want to count them all messages, to church pastors and leaders asking that they view my site and pray. No one else has responded.

I answered an ad in the paper that requested a worship leader for a denominational church. We talked and I shared about the books and my web site. I was open and honest and willing to share, as I am filled with excitement about what God is doing. We discussed that I could play the keyboard as well as sing and I auditioned.

He asked that I attend his church service for two weeks while he had a chance to pray. I did so and while I was there I moved in the Holy Spirit as I do and he acknowledged publicly that there was a great difference in the worship service that day for the better.

I needed to email him and ask what his intentions were as I had not gotten a response as promised at the appointed time. When I did I asked that he view my web site and pray and see if there would be an opening for me to be a guest minister in his denomination pointing out the mission described on my site.

He responded with a long series of instructions that I needed to follow if I wanted any help from him. Even though my credentials are clearly laid out in my books and on my site and the fact that he acknowledged that the Holy Spirit anointing was upon me he still required the following:

That I attend his church and submit to him as the pastor and let them evaluate me over a long period of time. I was required to be in submission to him as a pastor even though he knew but obviously forgot that I have a pastor. He could not allow his name to be associated with my ministry and could not offer any direction as I requested. He ended with this offer; "I was welcome to attend his church." Sorry, I deleted his email because I was so upset or I could have given you a more precise version of his words. I will never know if he bothered to look at my site. I feel that he is so structured in religion he didn't even bother to consider that God may be speaking to him through this woman of; "NO VALUE?"

My response to his email included renditions of: "New wine does not fit in old wine skins" & "God has the prerogative to move as He pleases."

What does this have to do with transparency? God wants to bring a revival renewing relationship with Him. This requires that the church at large meaning denominations etc. tear down the walls of their particular claim to fame in Him and be real.

Example: If someone enters your space and confronts on a level in which you are not accustom rather than retreat into your set of rules, LIVE A LITTLE! Maybe, you are experiencing a divine visitation like Mary in the Bible. Maybe, there are angels being dismissed unaware. Maybe, God did not write all your rules. Maybe, He wants to be invited into His church. Maybe, He can do far above what we think. Maybe, we need to get out of His way.

Bottom line concerning the current "Revelation of Transparency" is as follows: God needs an environment of transparency further explained as a living and dynamic relationship between God and His people and one another in which He can move to renew His church for the challenges ahead.

About the Author

Barbara is the mother of four children who are prospering in fields of success. They are followed by four grandchildren who are all filled with potential. She has an associates and Bible college degree. She taught in a Christian school, ministered in the streets as an evangelist, orchestrated a dynamic prophetic prayer group to victories for the nations and is now taking off as an author. Her most influential teacher is the Holy Spirit who has led her through life.